Christoffel Pattern Coloring Book

Stefan Hollos and J. Richard Hollos

Christoffel Pattern Coloring Book
by Stefan Hollos and J. Richard Hollos
Ebook ISBN 978-1-887187-25-1

Copyright ©2014 by Exstrom Laboratories LLC

Abrazol Publishing

an imprint of Exstrom Laboratories LLC
662 Nelson Park Drive, Longmont, CO 80503-7674 U.S.A.

About the patterns in this book

Most of the patterns in this book are based on Christoffel words, named after Elwin Bruno Christoffel (1829-1900), a German mathematician and physicist. Details on pattern generation with Christoffel words can be found in our book "Pattern Generation for Computational Art".

There are 50 patterns in this book, each on its own physical page. Having one pattern per physical page reduces bleed-through of colors, and makes a cleaner photocopy.

1

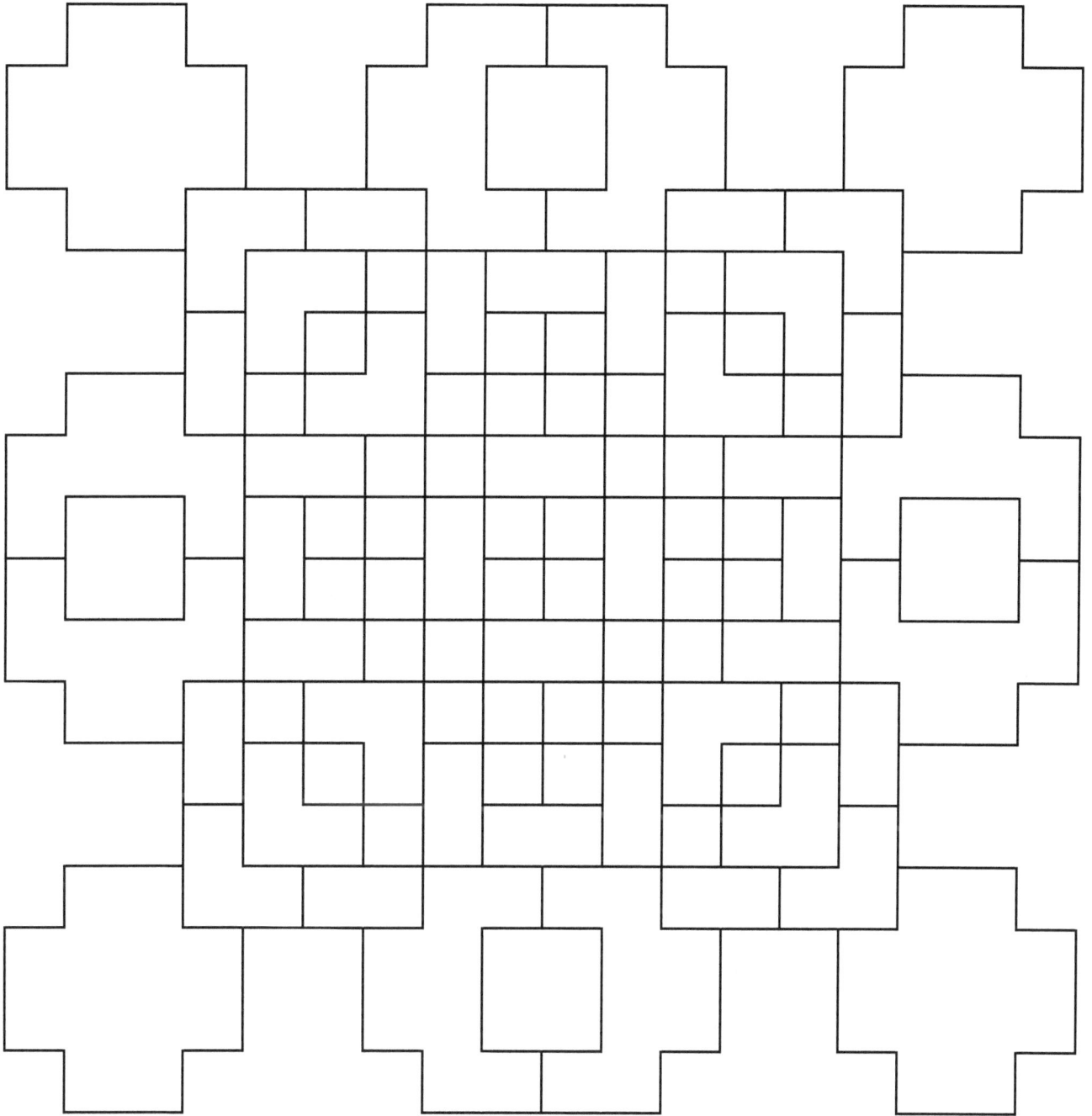

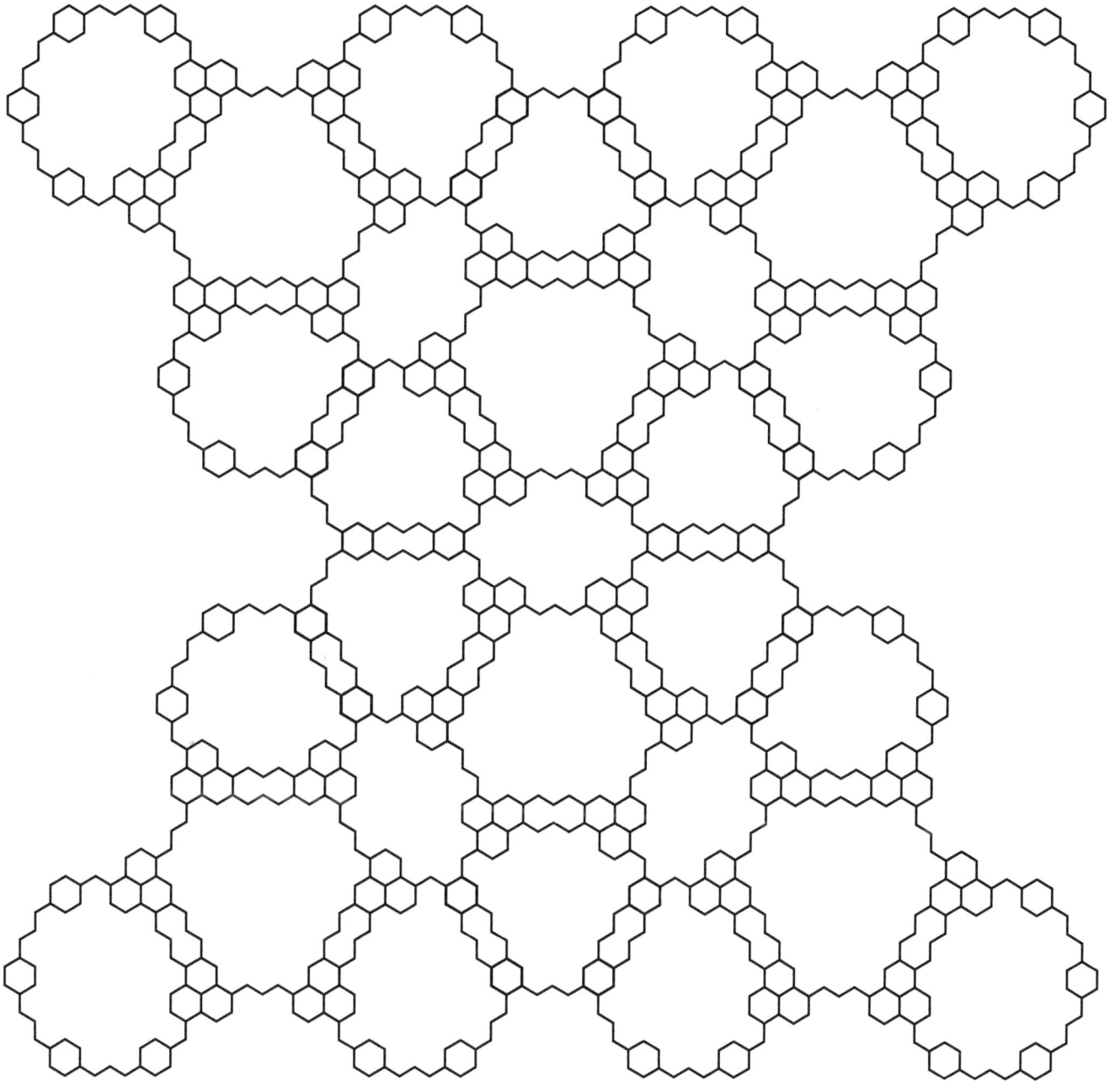

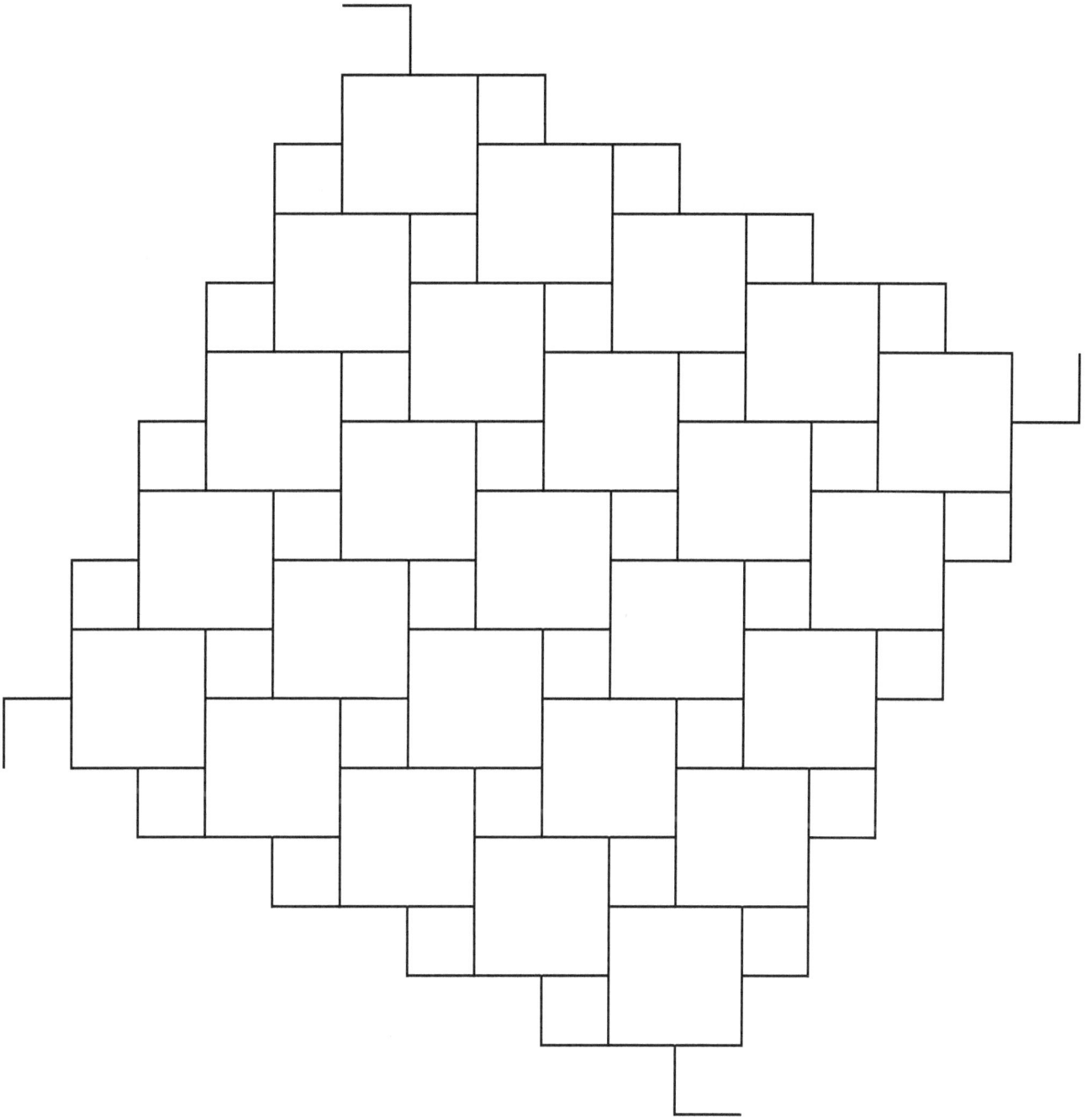

6

7

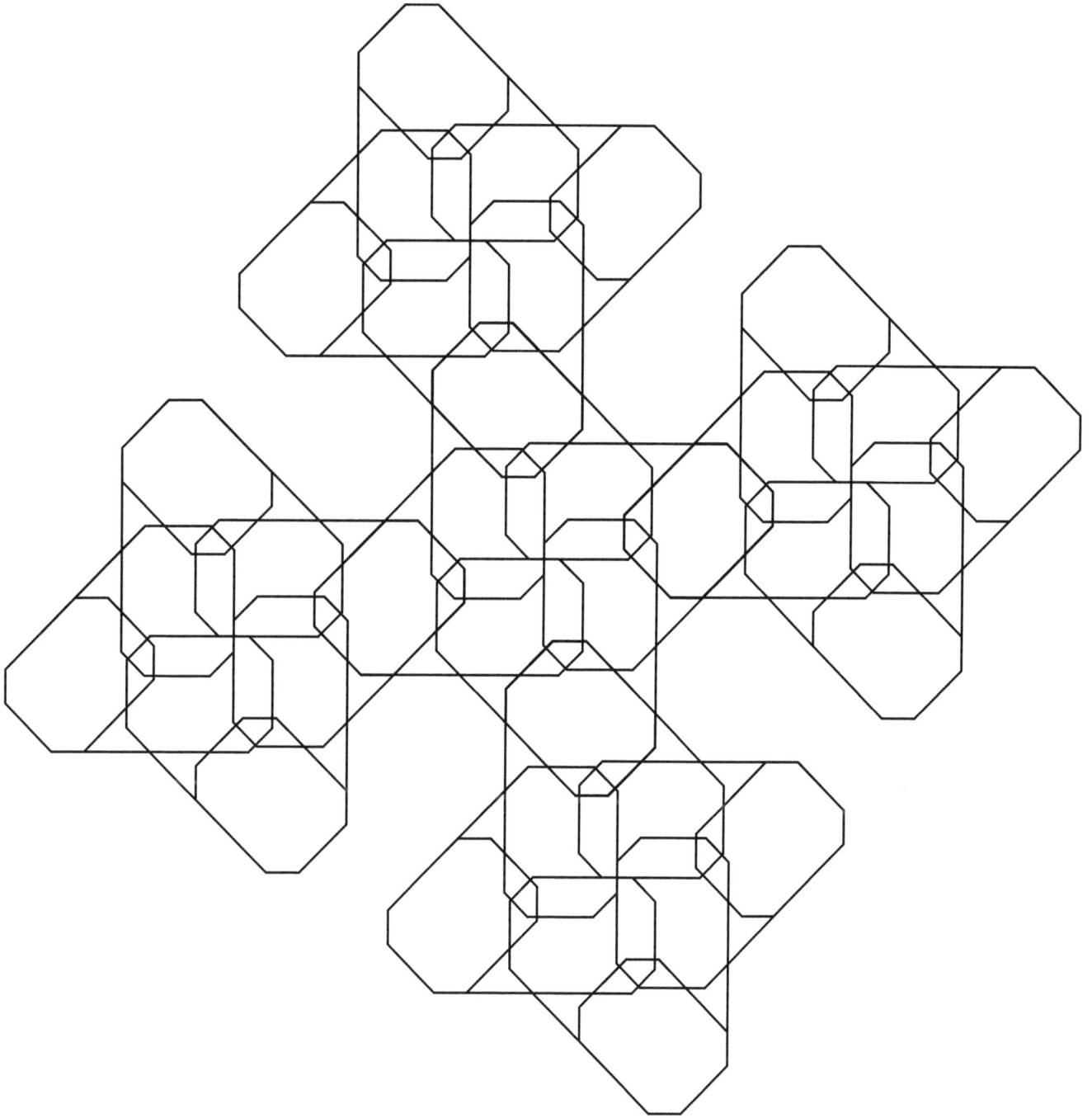

9

10

11

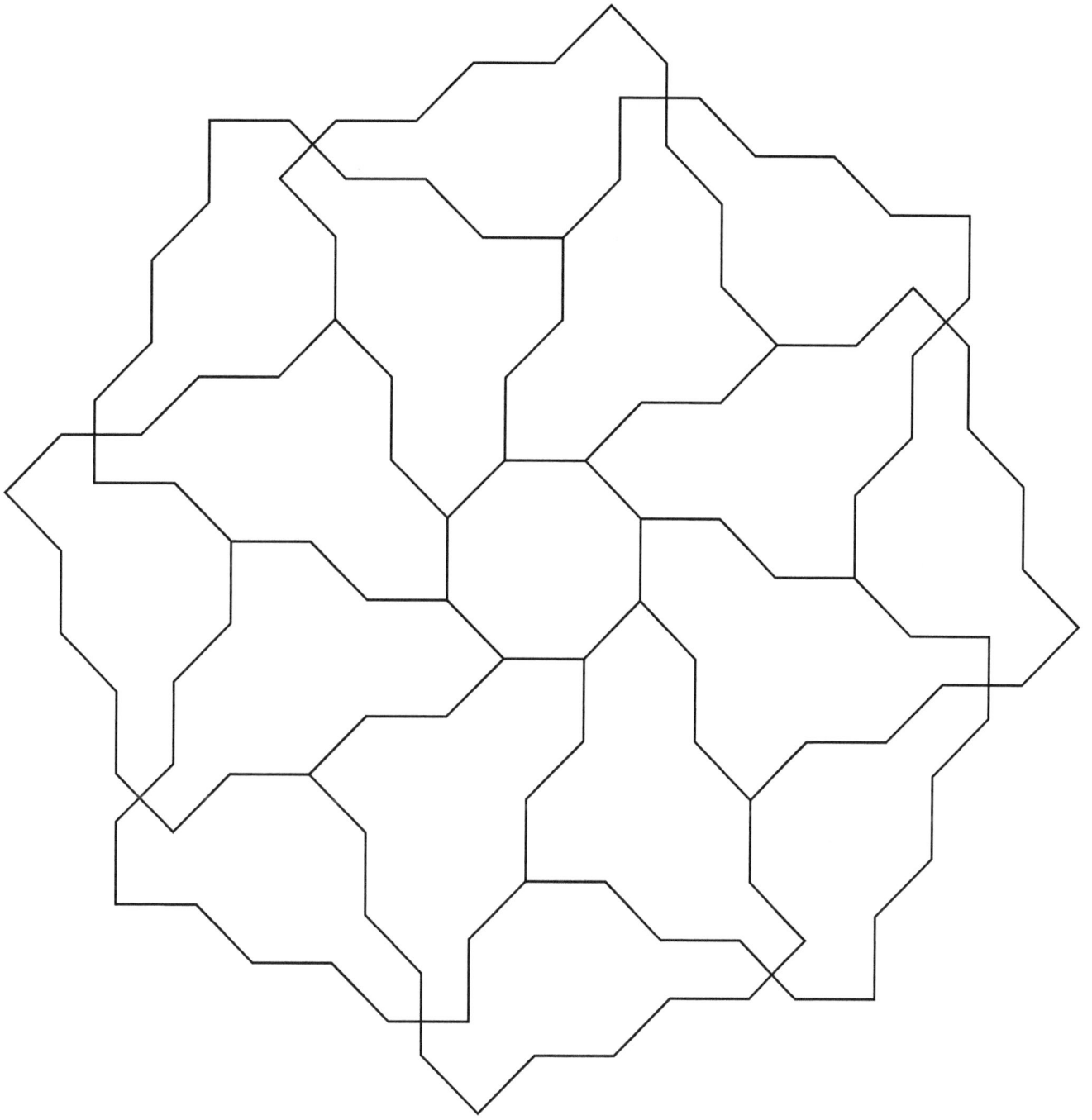

13

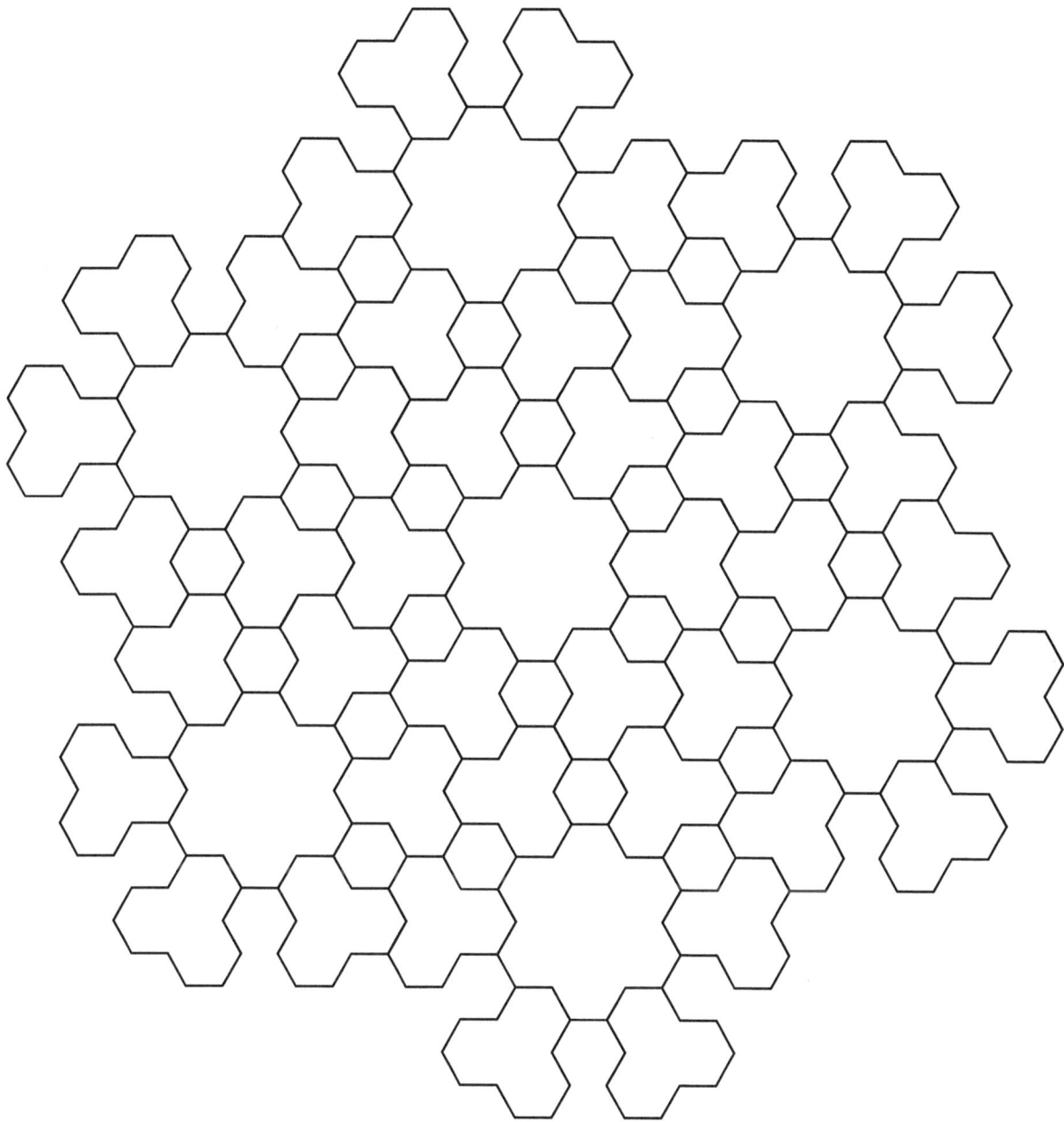

14

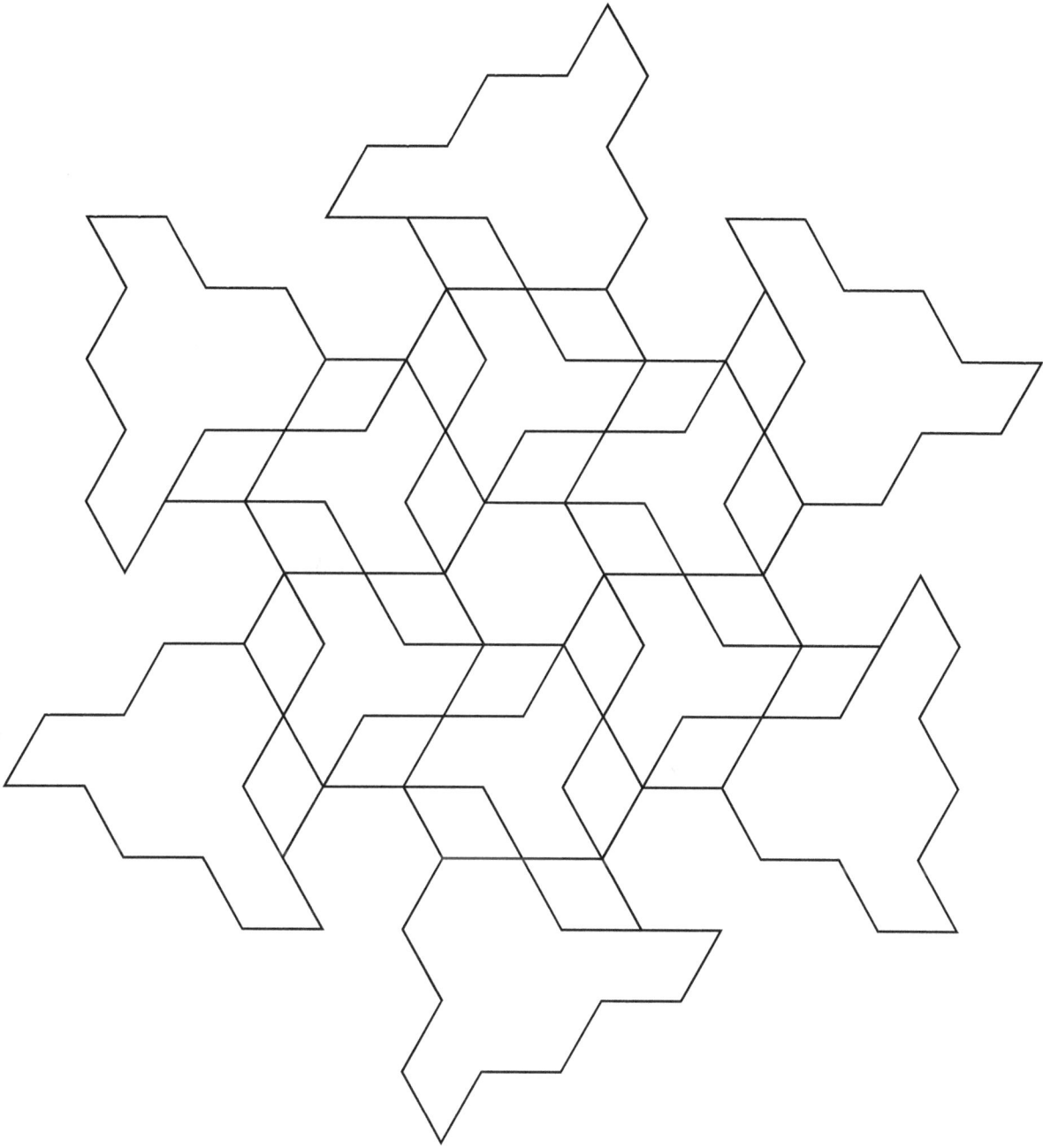

16

18

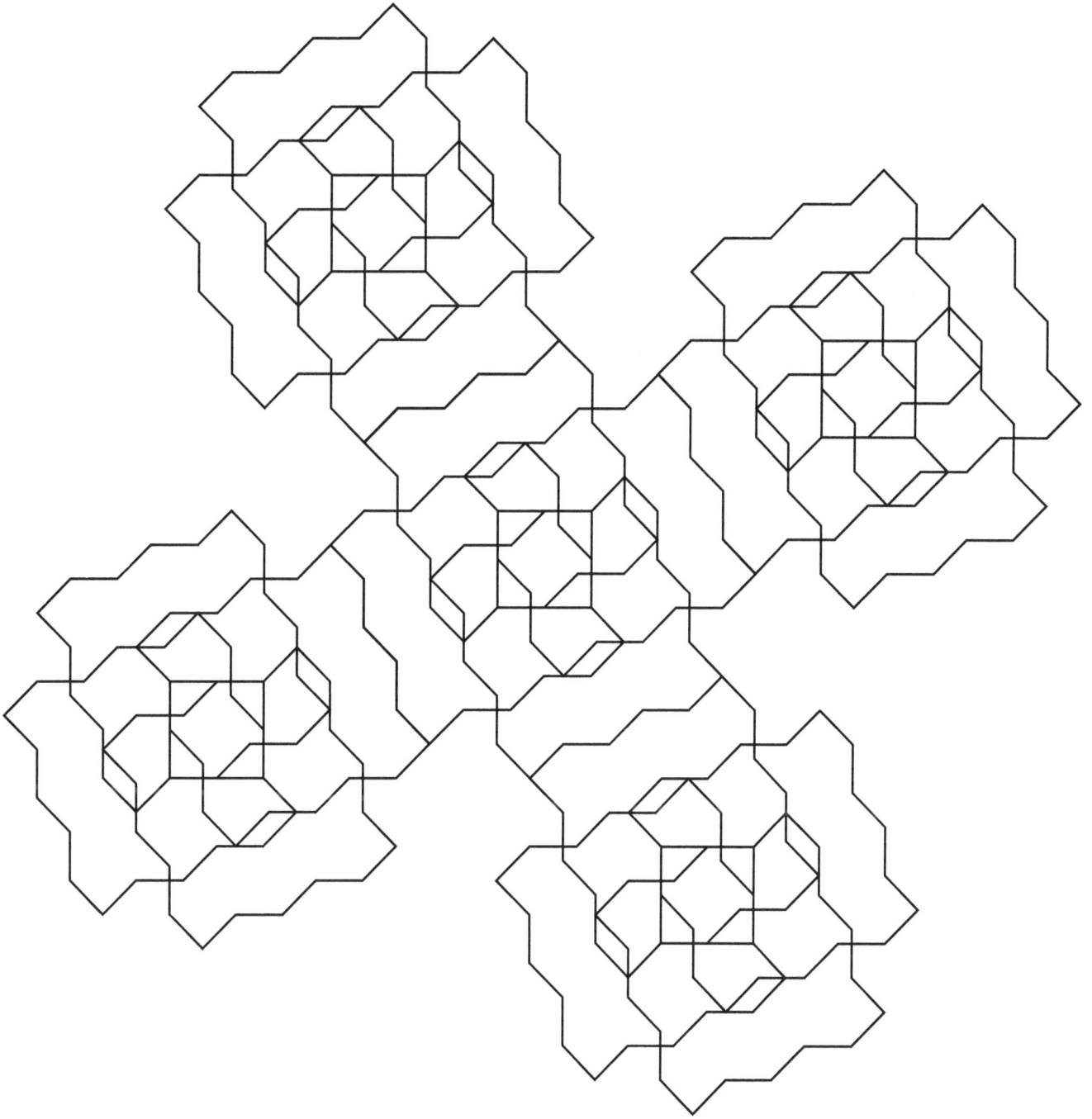

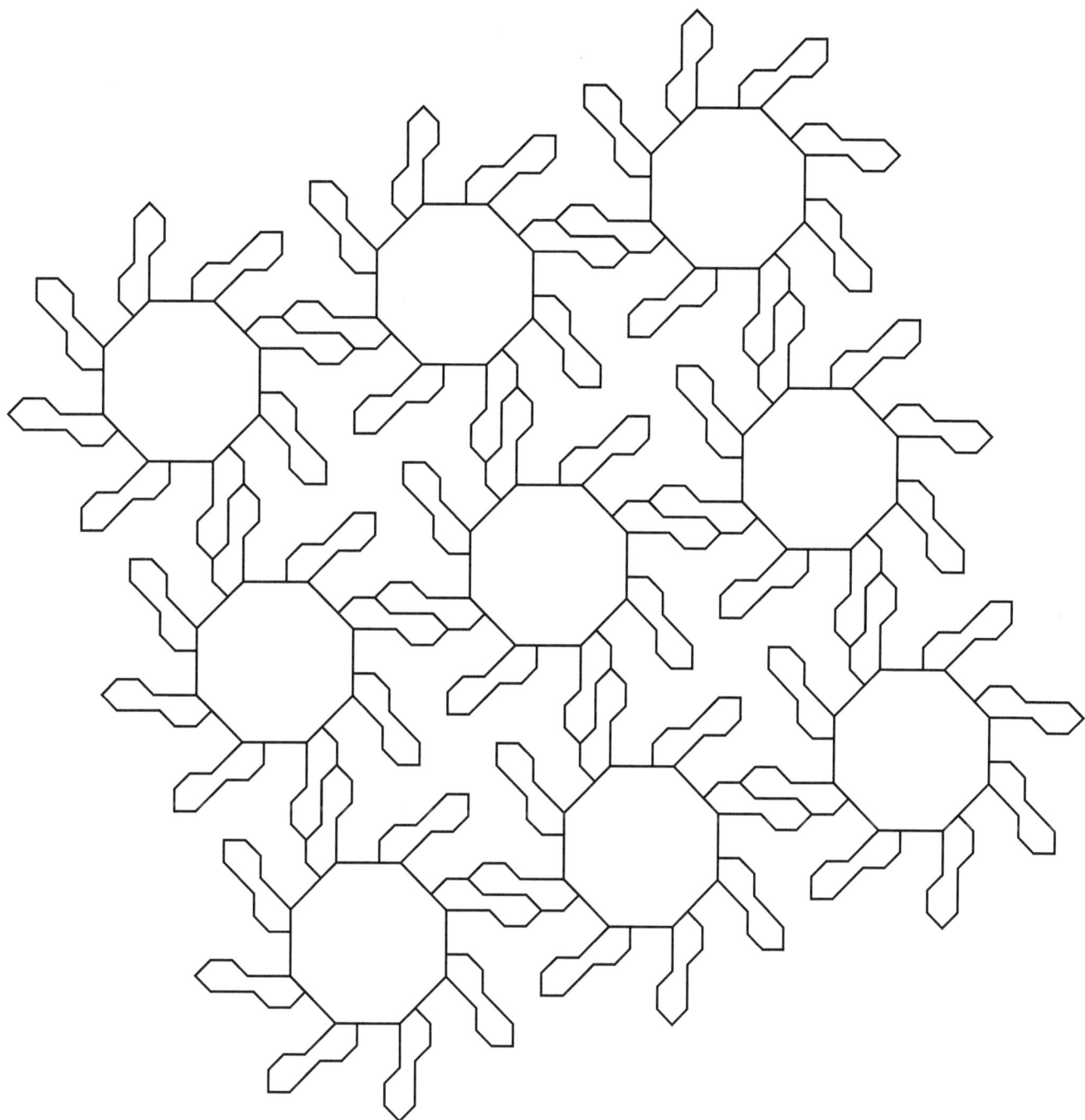

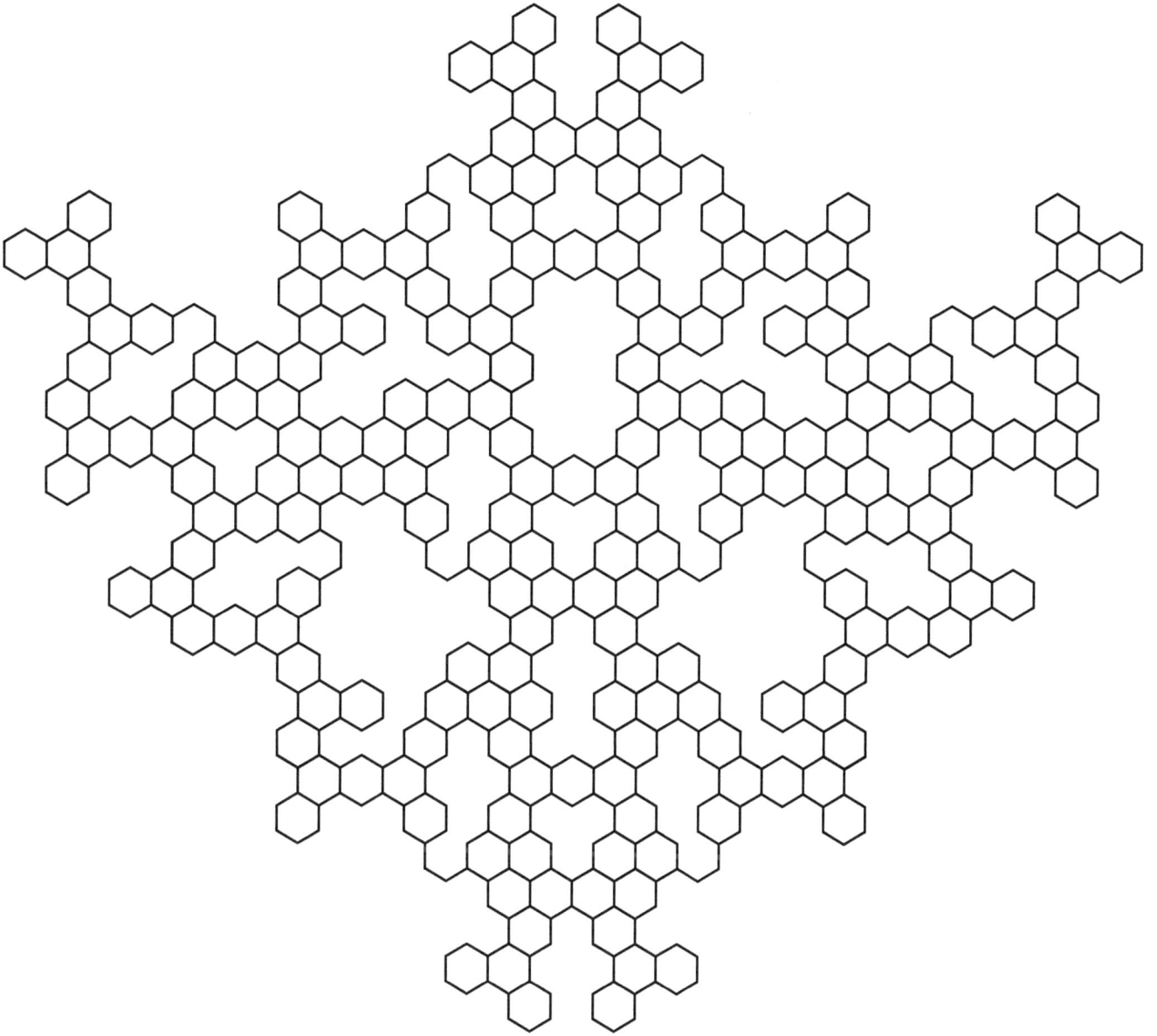

24

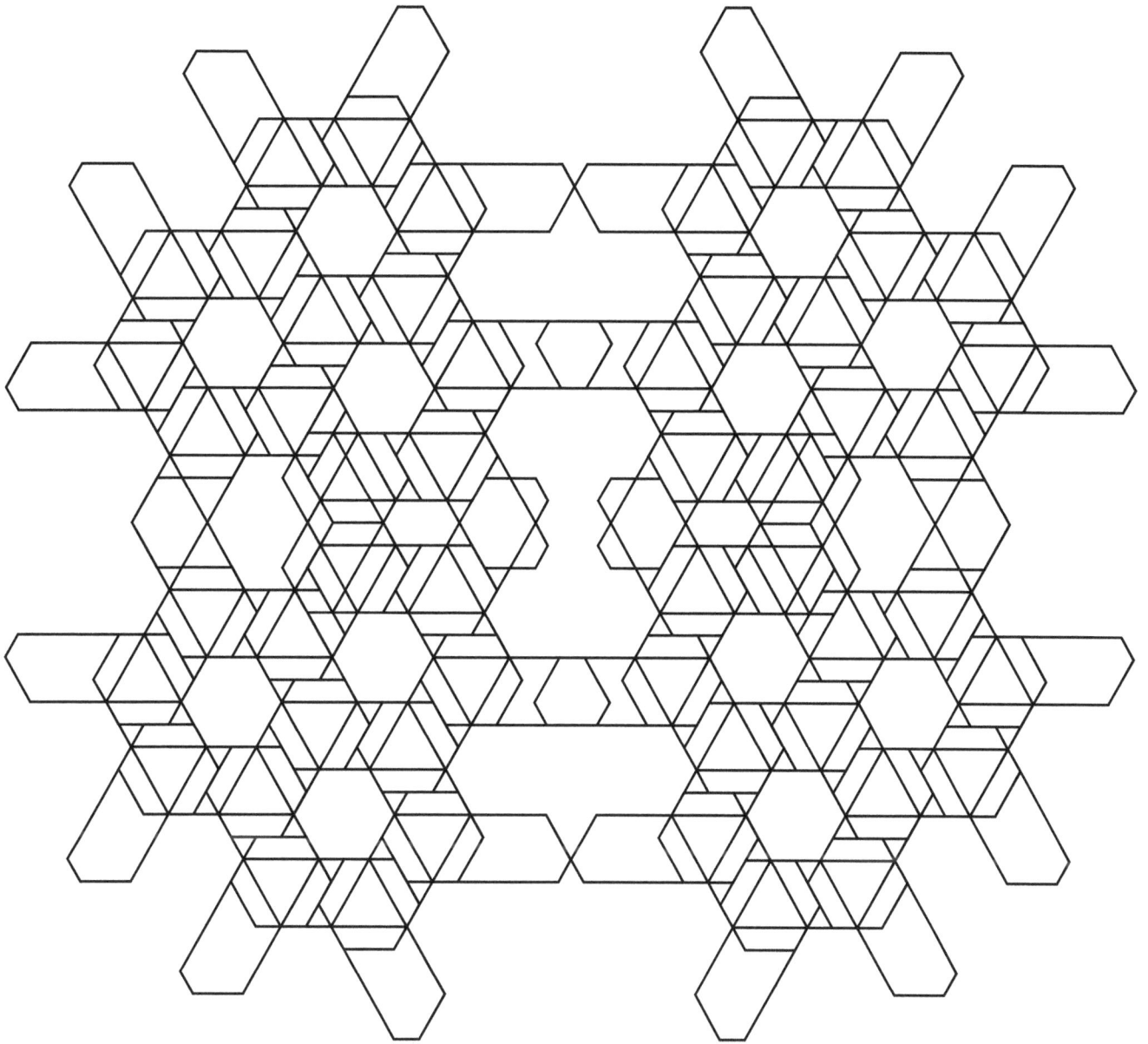

25

26

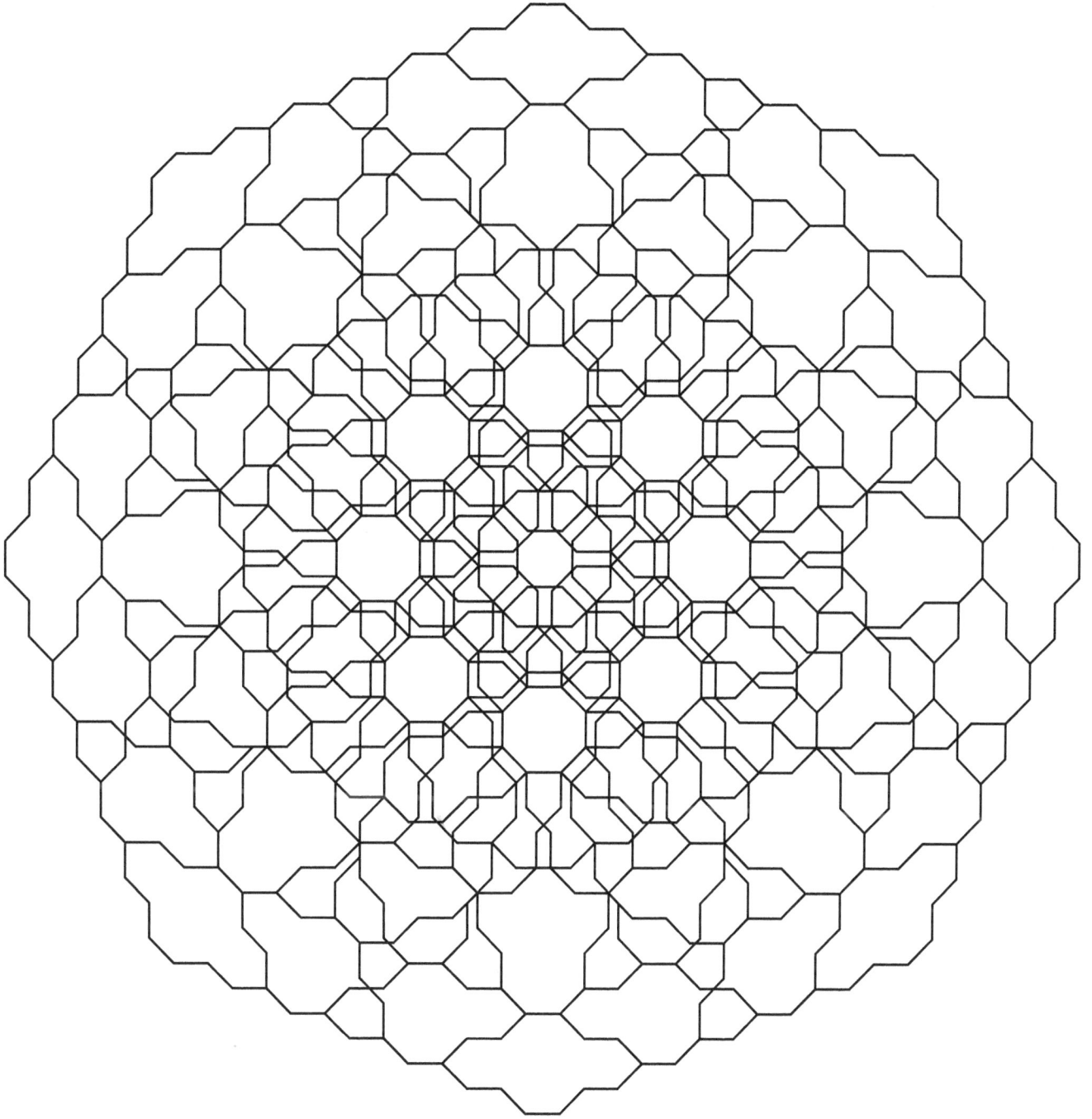

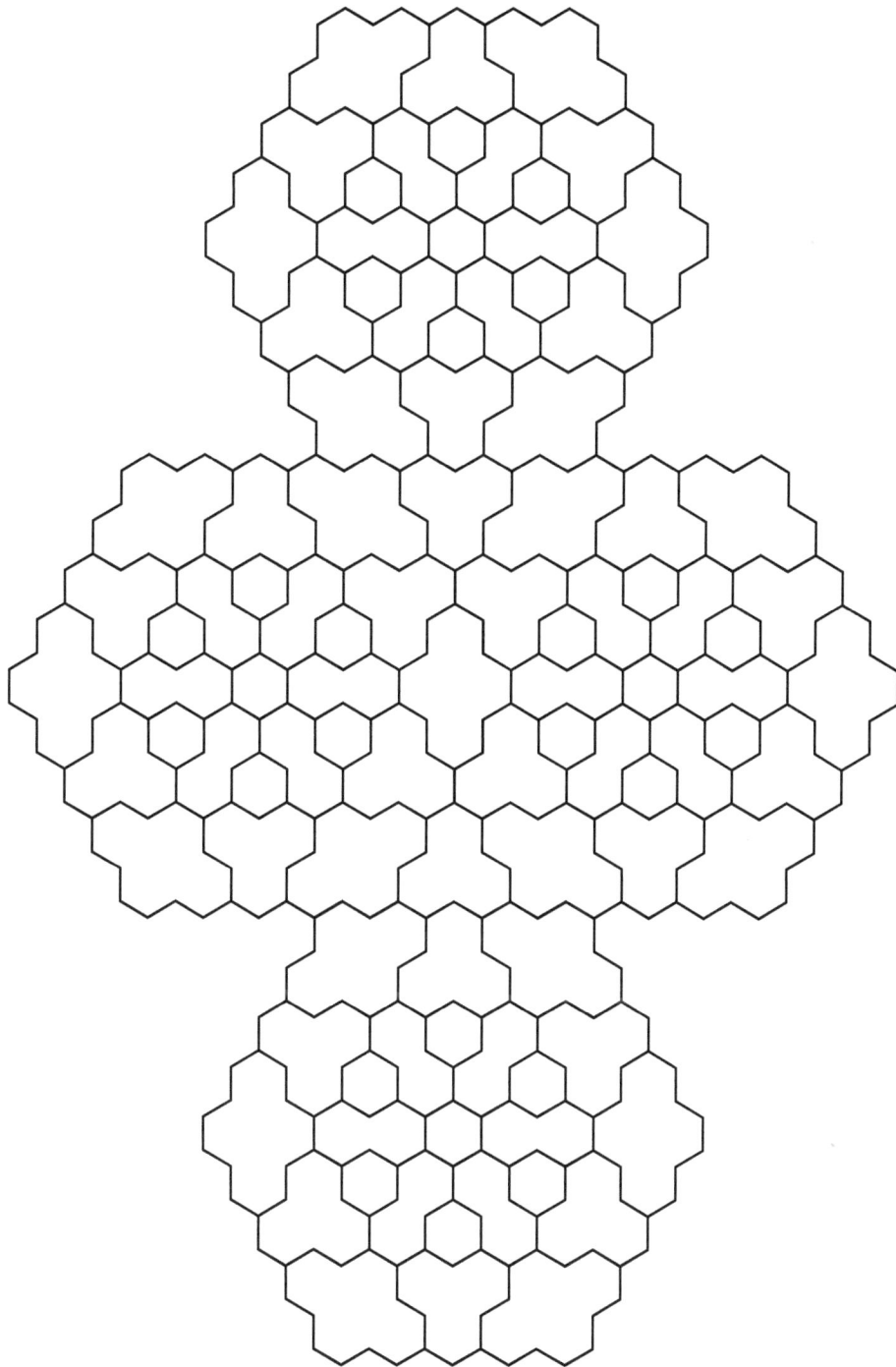

28

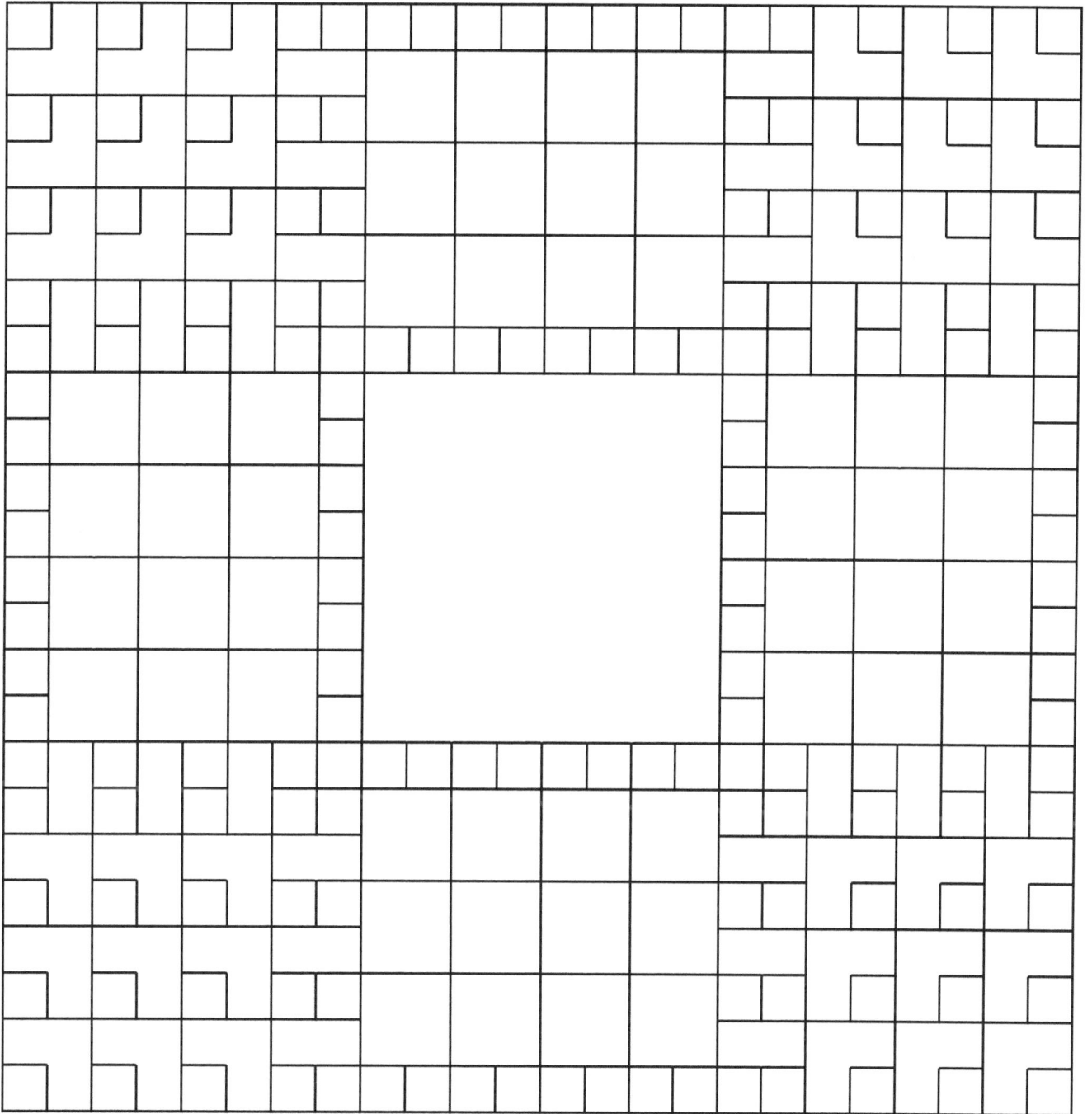

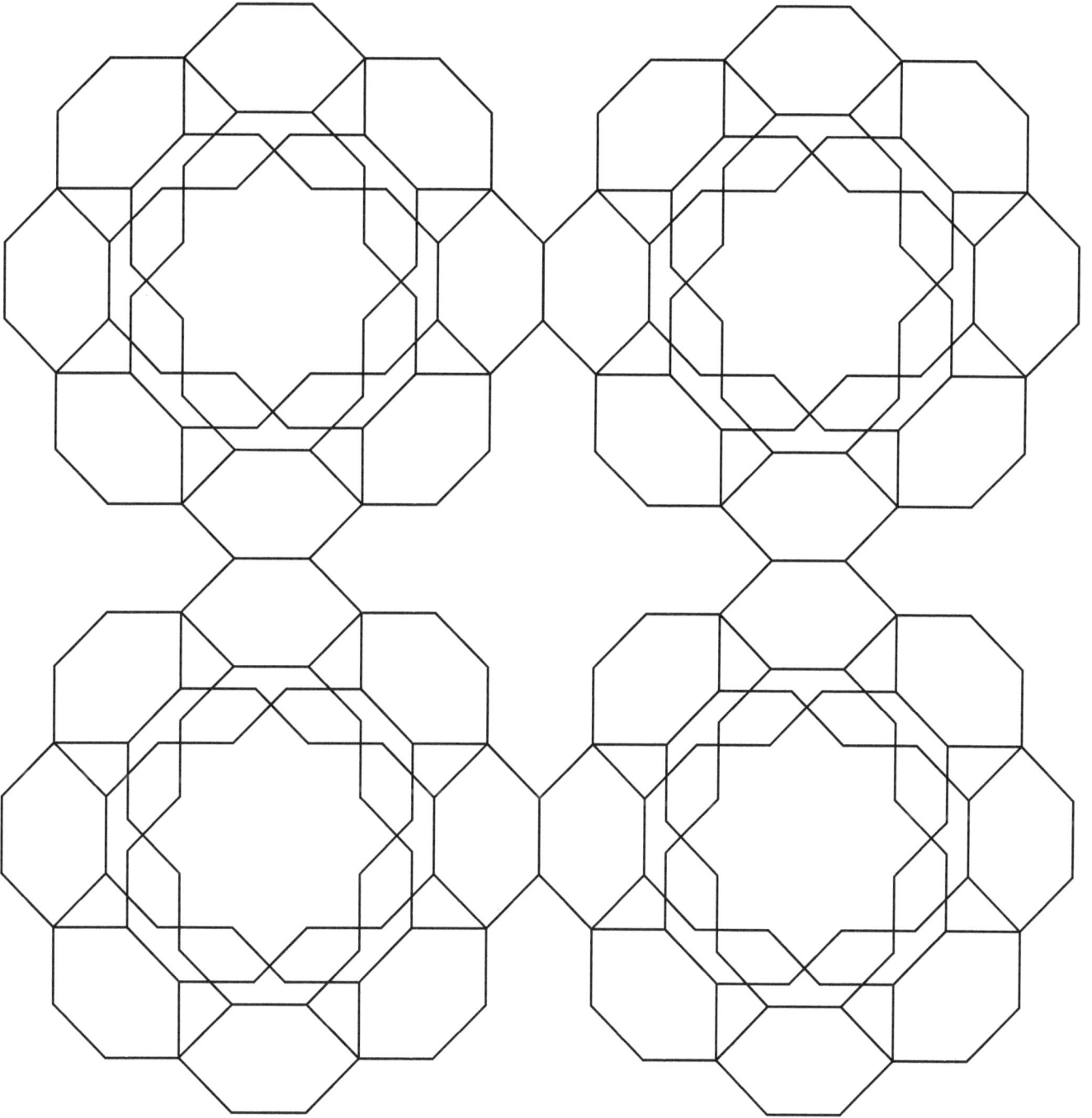

34

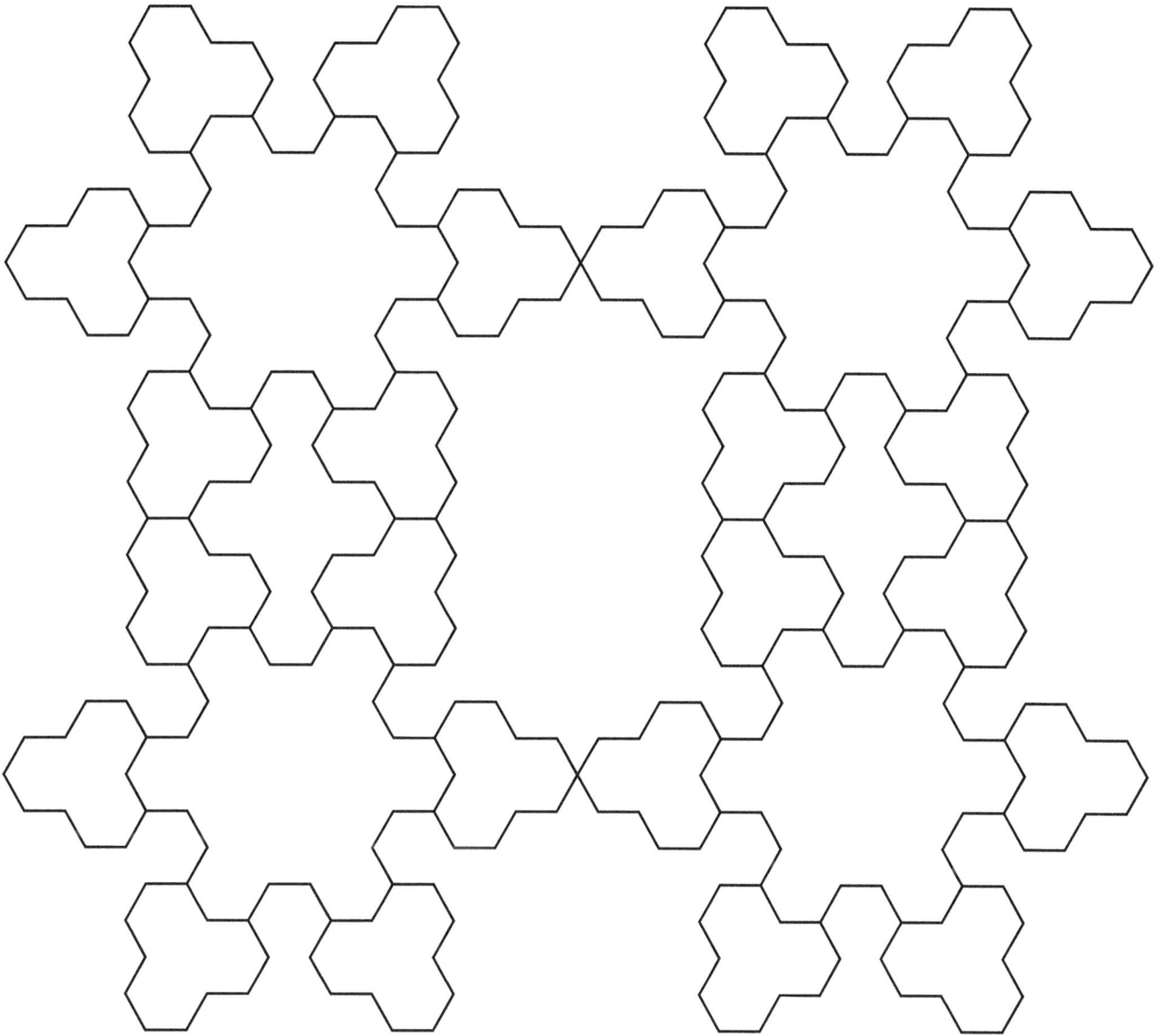

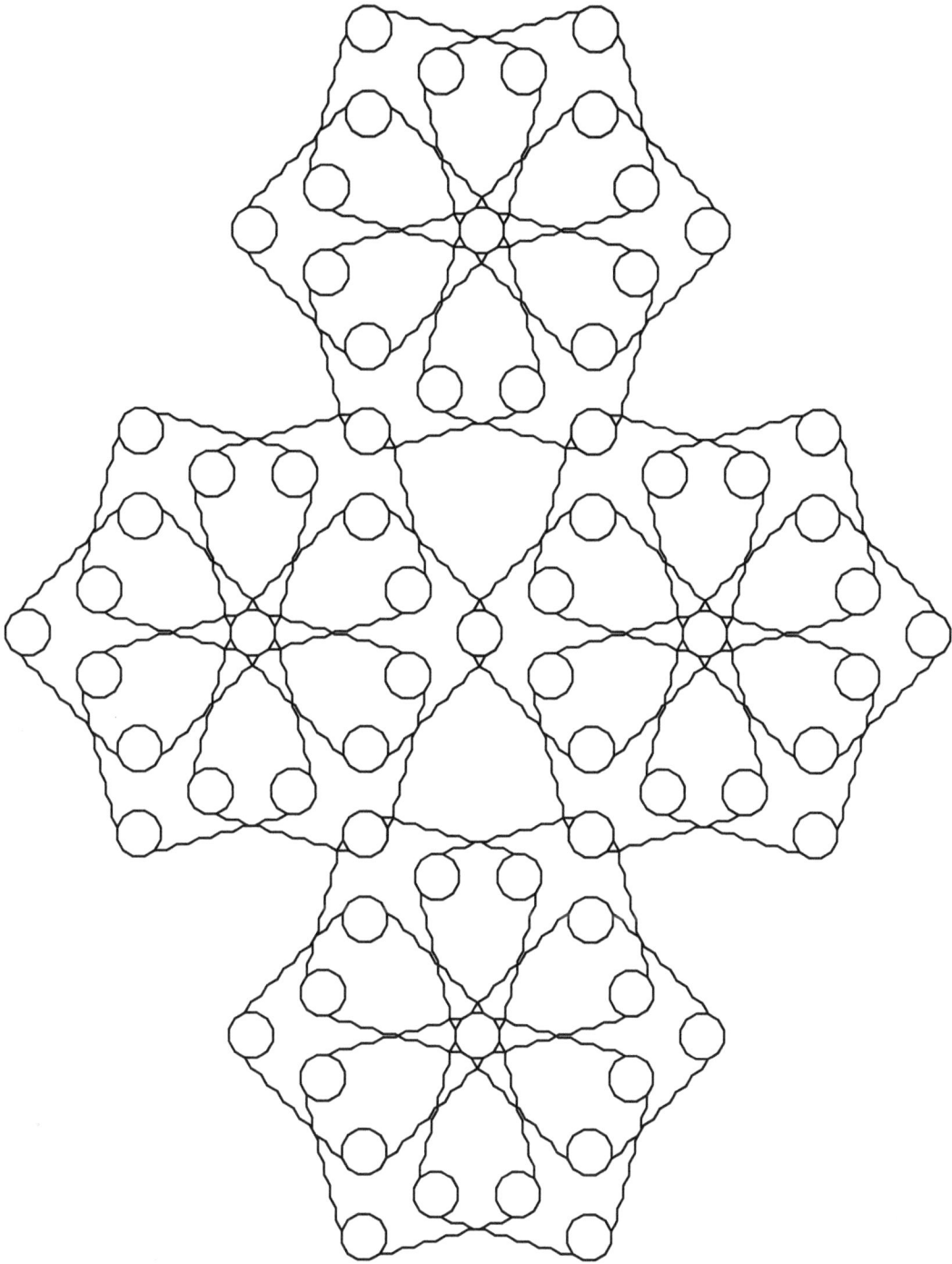

36

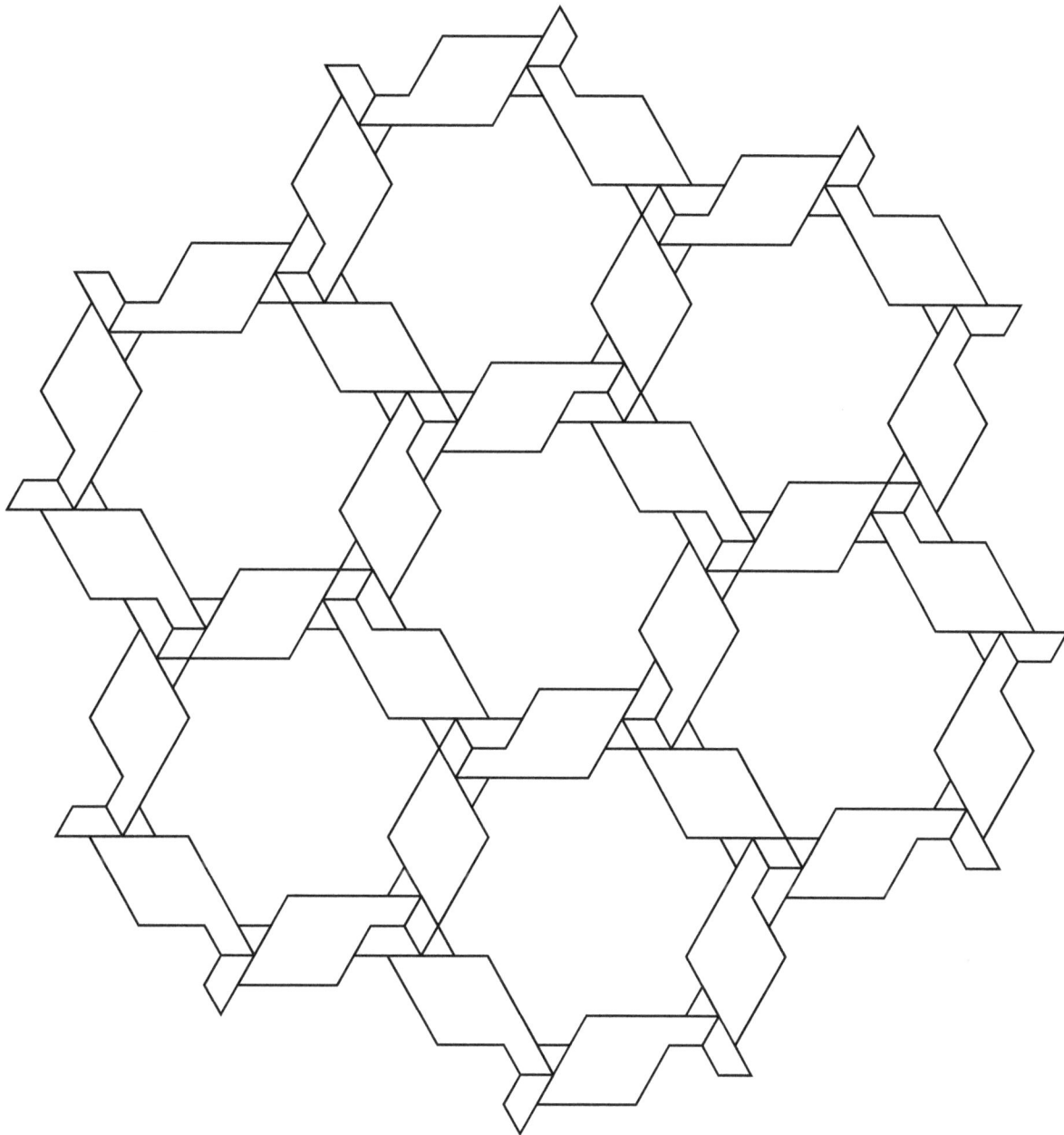

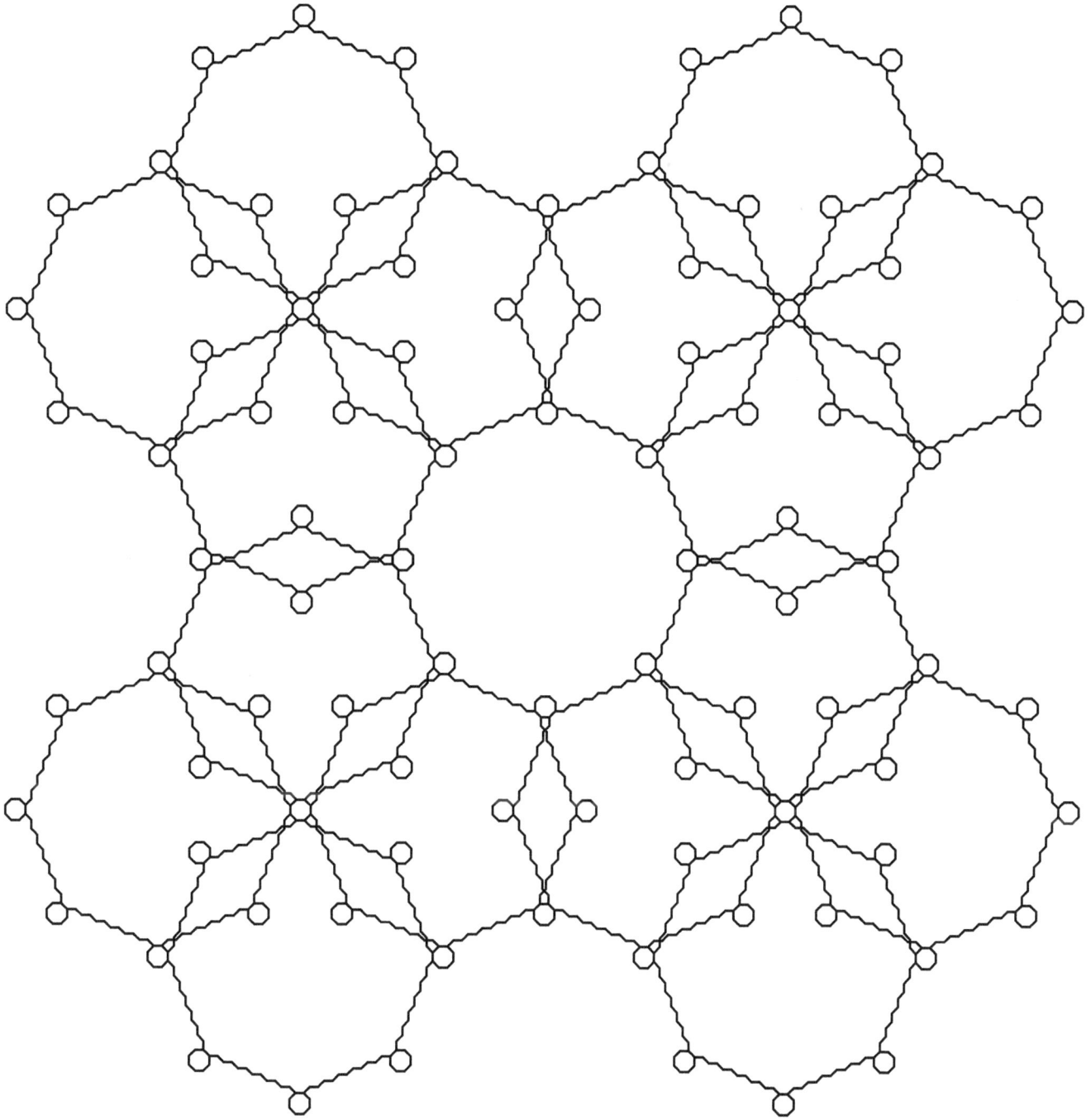

39

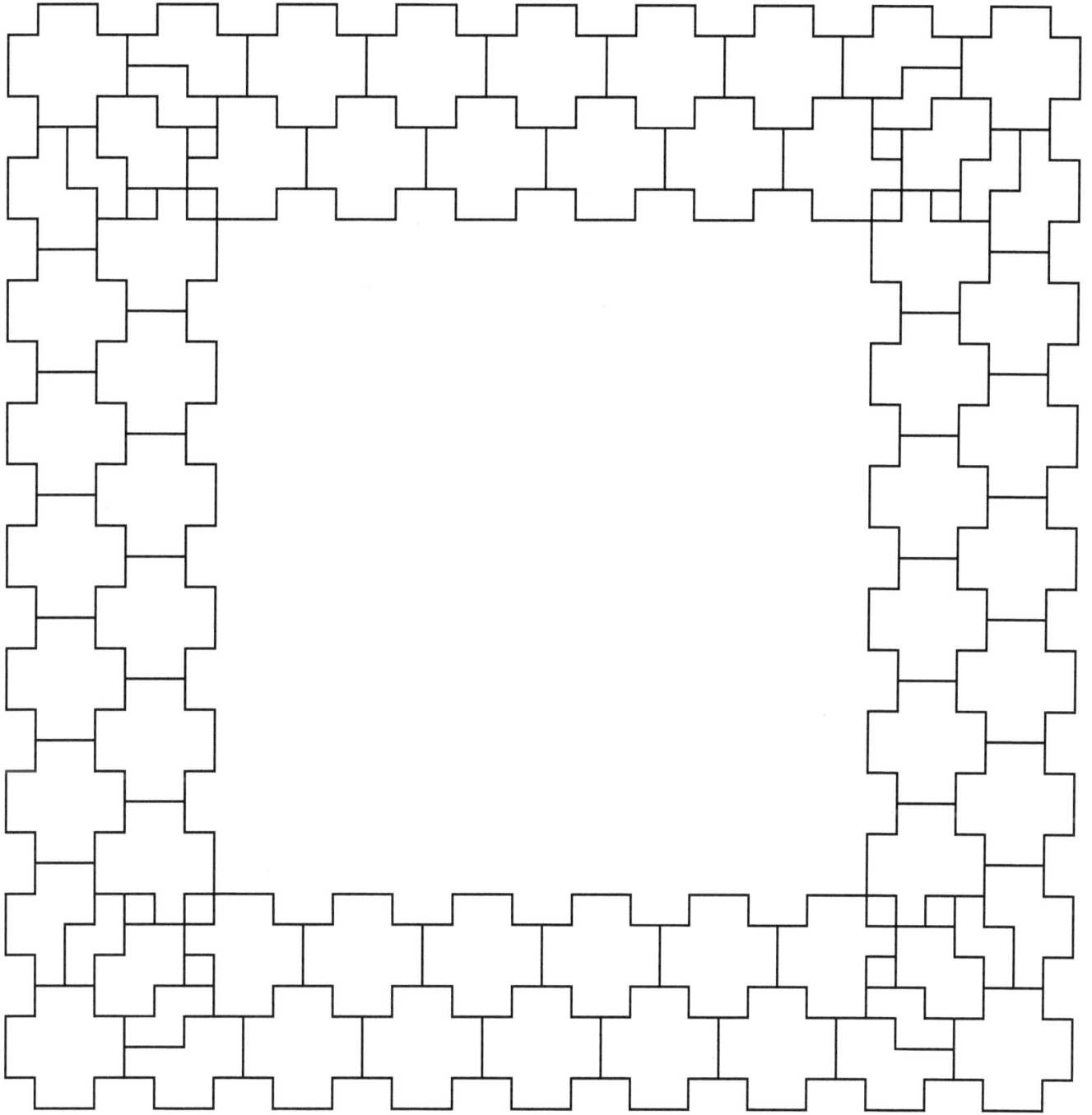

40

41

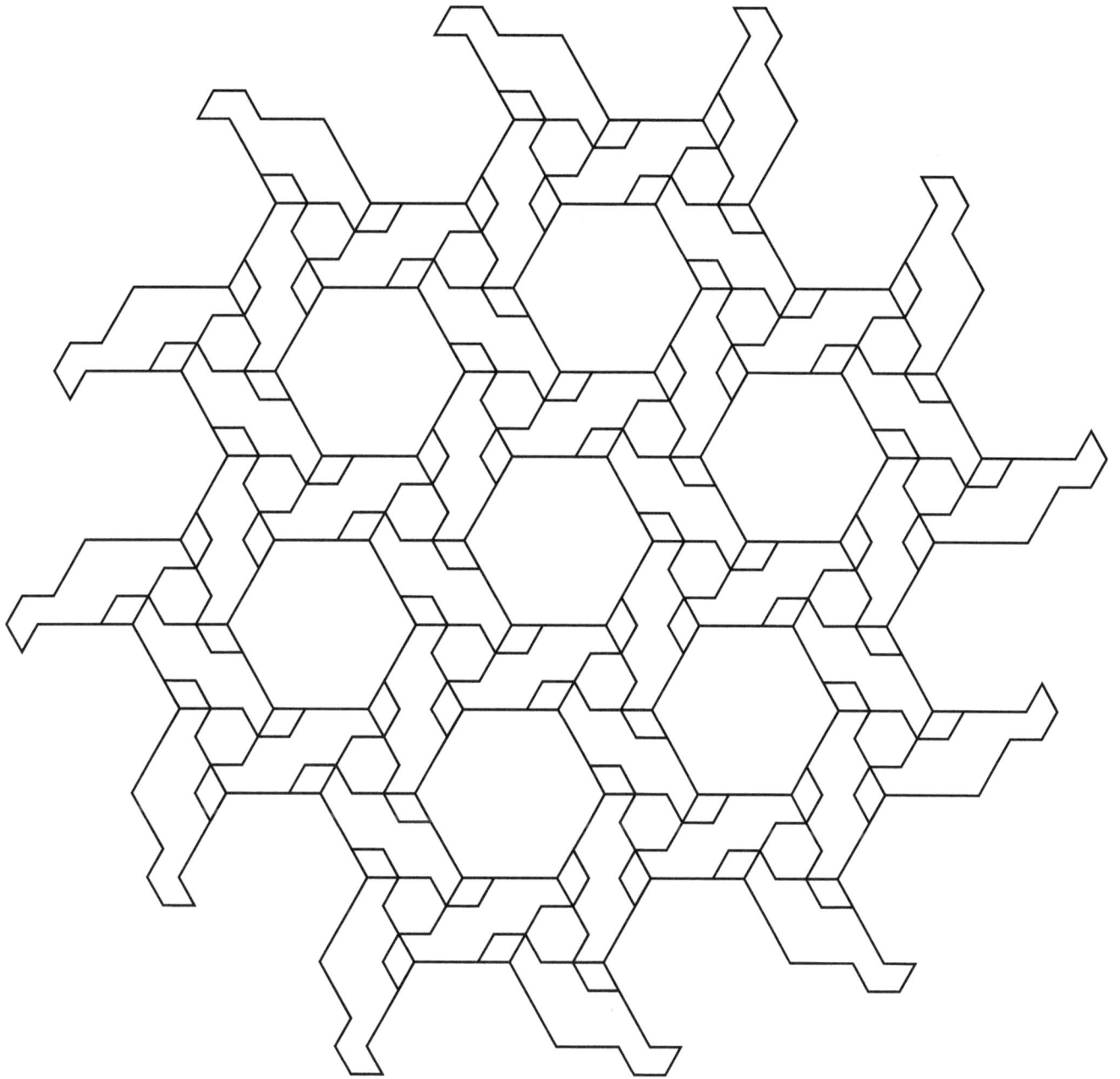

42

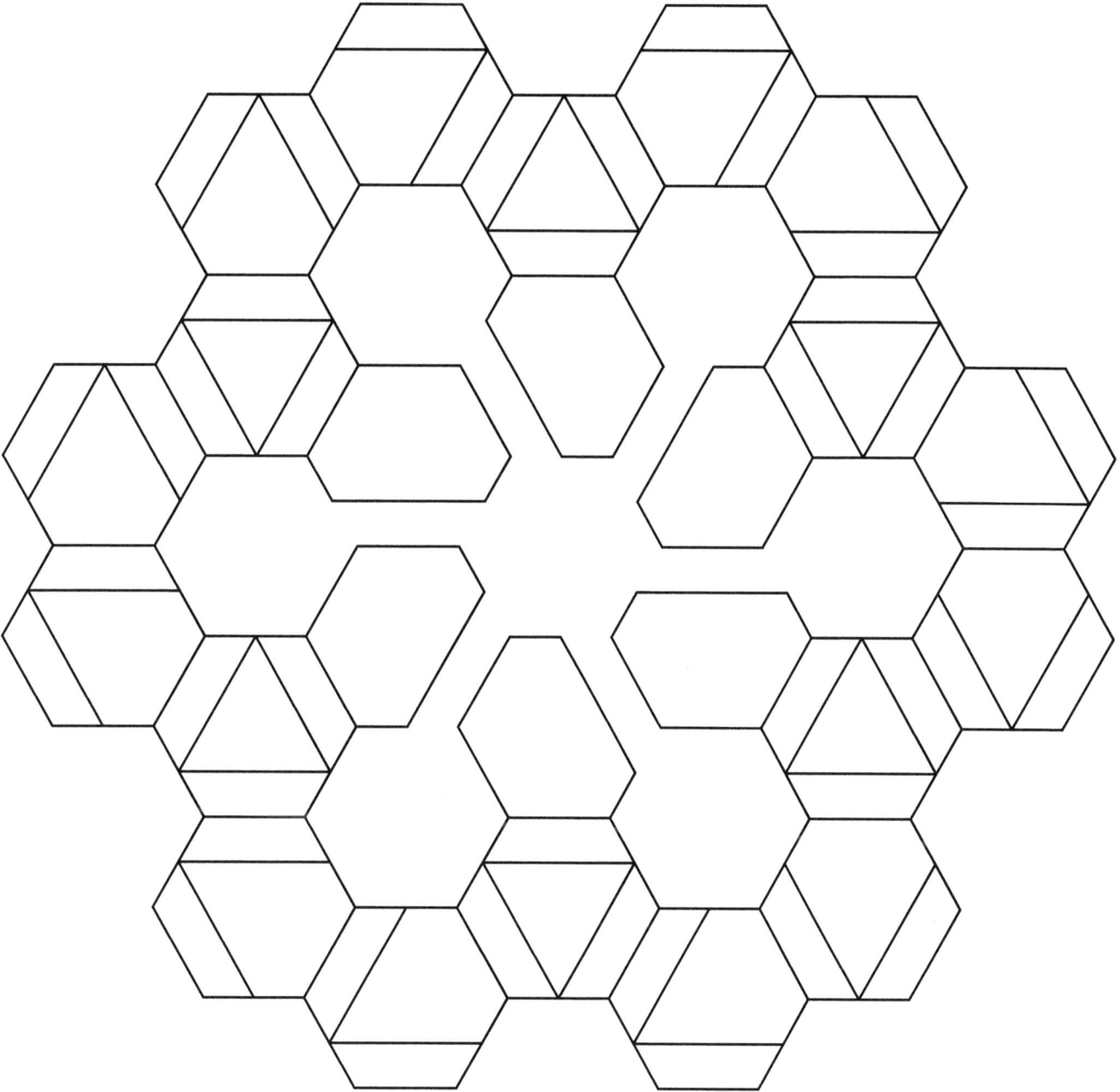

44

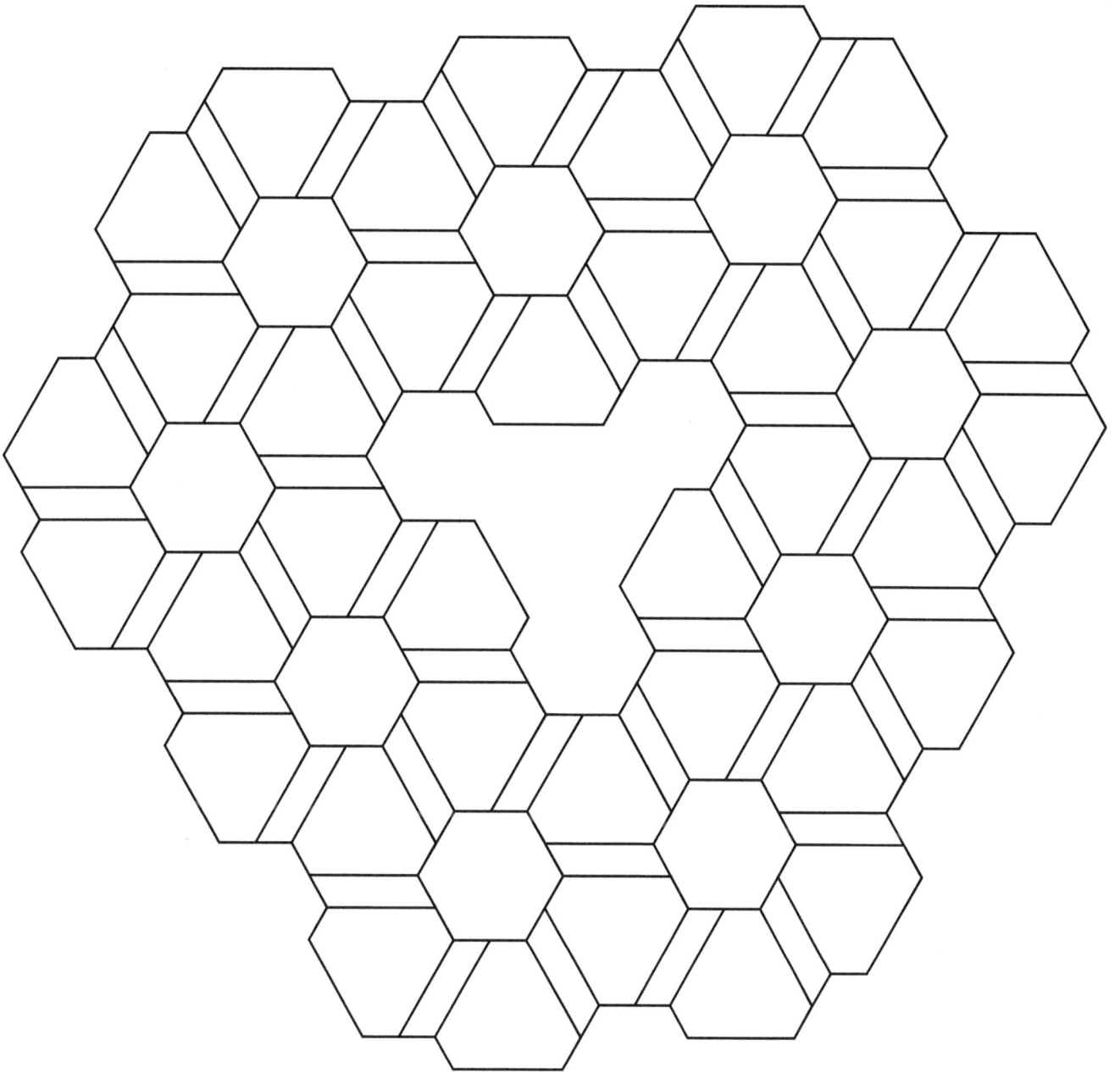

46

47

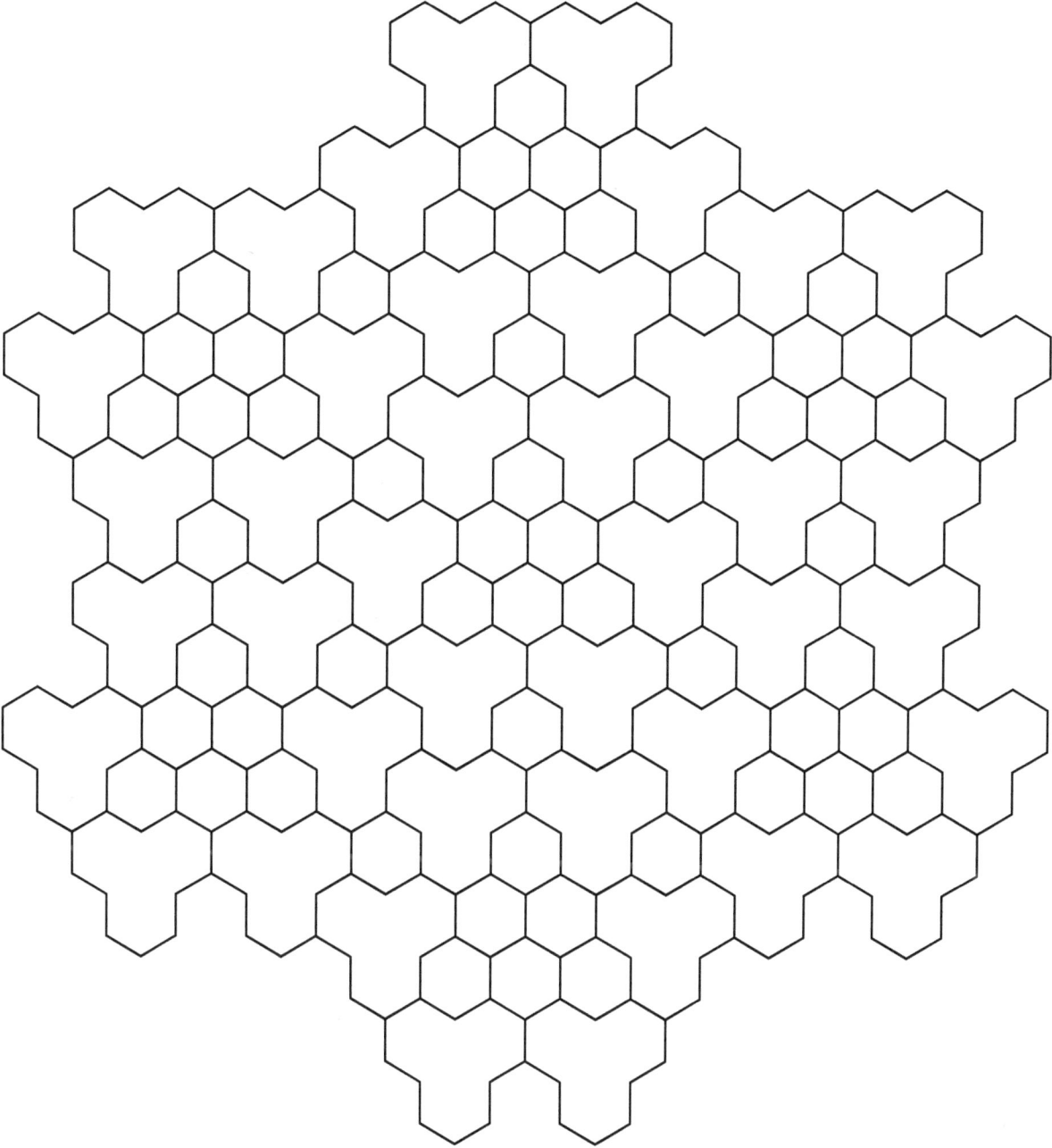

50

Thank You

Thank you for buying this book.

Sign up for the Abrazol Publishing Newsletter and receive news on new editions, new products, and special offers. Just go to

http://www.abrazol.com/

and enter your email address.

www.ingramcontent.com/pod-product-compliance
Lightning Source LLC
Chambersburg PA
CBHW081659270326
41933CB00017B/3219